The
BIRTHDAY
BOOK

Dates to Remember Every Year

This book belongs to:

....

....

January

* * *

January Birth Flower: Carnation & Snowdrop

January Birthstone: Garnet

Capricorn (Goat): 22 Dec – 19 Jan

patient, hardworking, smart

Aquarius (Water Bearer): 20 Jan – 18 Feb

accepting, happy, unconventional

1

2

3

4

5

6

7

8

9

10

11

12

13

14

15

16

17

18

19

20

21

22

23

24

25

26

27

28

29

30

31

February

* * *

February Birth Flower: Violet & Primrose

February Birthstone: Amethyst

Aquarius (Water Bearer): 20 Jan – 18 Feb

accepting, happy, unconventional

Pisces (Fish): 19 Feb – 20 Mar

brave, emphatic, devoted

1

2

3

4

5

6

7

8

9

10

11

12

13

14

15

16

17

18

19

20

21

22

23

24

25

26

27

28

29

March

* * *

March Birth Flower: Daffodil or Jonquil

March Birthstone: Aquamarine

Pisces (Fish): 19 Feb – 20 Mar

brave, emphatic, devoted

Aries (Ram): 21 Mar – 19 Apr

spontaneous, open, idealistic

1

2

3

4

5

6

7

8

9

10

11

12

13

14

15

16

17

18

19

20

21

22

23

24

25

26

27

28

29

30

31

April

* * *

April Birth Flower: Daisy & Sweet Pea

April Birthstone: Diamond

Aries (Ram): 21 Mar – 19 Apr

spontaneous, open, idealistic

Taurus (Bull): 20 Apr – 20 May

caring, insightful, sensual

1

2

3

4

5

6

7

8

9

10

11

12

13

14

15

16

17

18

19

20

21

22

23

24

25

26

27

28

29

30

May

* * *

May Birth Flower: Lily of the Valley & Hawthorn

May Birthstone: Emerald

Taurus (Bull): 20 Apr – 20 May

caring, insightful, sensual

Gemini (Twins): 21 May – 21 Jun

lively, flexible, energetic

1

2

3

4

5

6

7

8

9

10

11

12

13

14

15

16

17

18

19

20

21

22

23

24

25

26

27

28

29

30

31

June

* * *

June Birth Flower: Rose & Honeysuckle

June Birthstone: Pearl or moonstone

Gemini (Twins): 21 May – 21 Jun

lively, flexible, energetic

Cancer (Crab): 22 Jun – 22 Jul

unusual, compassionate, sensitive

1

2

3

4

5

6

7

8

9

10

11

12

13

14

15

16

17

18

19

20

21

22

23

24

25

26

27

28

29

30

July

* * *

July Birth Flower: Larkspur & Water lily

July Birthstone: Ruby

Cancer (Crab): 22 Jun – 22 Jul

unusual, compassionate, sensitive

Leo (Lion): 23 Jul – 22 Aug

loyal, confident, big-hearted

1

2

3

4

5

6

7

8

9

10

11

12

13

14

15

16

17

18

19

20

21

22

23

24

25

26

27

28

29

30

31

August

* * *

August Birth Flower: Gladiolus & Poppy

August Birthstone: Peridot

Leo (Lion): 23 Jul – 22 Aug

loyal, confident, big-hearted

Virgo (Virgin): 23 Aug – 22 Sept

generous, precise, humble

1

2

3

4

5

6

7

8

9

10

11

12

13

14

15

16

17

18

19

20

21

22

23

24

25

26

27

28

29

30

31

September

***

September Birth Flower: Aster & Morning Glory

September Birthstone: Sapphire

Virgo (Virgin): 23 Aug – 22 Sept

generous, precise, humble

Libra (Scales): 23 Sept – 23 Oct

thoughtful, energetic, fair

1

2

3

4

5

6

7

8

9

10

11

12

13

14

15

16

17

18

19

20

21

22

23

24

25

26

27

28

29

30

October

* * *

October Birth Flower: Marigold & Cosmos

October Birthstone: Opal

Libra (Scales): 23 Sept – 23 Oct

thoughtful, energetic, fair

Scorpio (Scorpion): 24 Oct – 22 Nov

powerful, sexual, serious

1

2

3

4

5

6

7

8

9

10

11

12

13

14

15

16

17

18

19

20

21

22

23

24

25

26

27

28

29

30

31

November

＊ ＊ ＊

November Birth Flower: Chrysanthemum

November Birthstone: Yellow Topaz

Scorpio (Scorpion): 24 Oct – 22 Nov

powerful, sexual, serious

Sagittarius (Archer): 23 Nov – 21 Dec

honest, optimistic, curious

1

2

3

4

5

6

7

8

9

10

11

12

13

14

15

16

17

18

19

20

21

22

23

24

25

26

27

28

29

30

December

* * *

December Birth Flower: Narcissus and Holly

December Birthstone: Blue Topaz/Turquoise

Sagittarius (Archer): 23 Nov – 21 Dec

honest, optimistic, curious

Capricorn (Goat): 22 Dec – 19 Jan

patient, hardworking, smart

1

2

3

4

5

6

7

8

9

10

11

12

13

14

15

16

17

18

19

20

21

22

23

24

25

26

27

28

29

30

31

Wedding Anniversary Gifts

First: Paper

Second: Cotton

Third: Leather

Fourth: Fruit/Flowers

Fifth: Wood

Sixth: Candy/Iron

Seventh: Wool/Copper

Eighth: Bronze/Pottery

Ninth: Pottery/Willow

Tenth: Tin/Aluminum

Eleventh: Steel

Twelfth: Silk/Linen

Thirteenth: Lace

Fourteenth: Ivory

Fifteenth: Crystal

Twentieth: China

Twenty-Fifth: Silver

Thirtieth: Pearl

Thirty-Fifth: Coral

Fortieth: Ruby

Forty-Fifth: Sapphire

Fiftieth: Gold

Fifty-Fifth: Emerald

Sixtieth: Diamond

Made in United States
Troutdale, OR
12/04/2024

25898033R00060